A LOVE THAT LASTS

Published by Hallmark Books,
a division of Hallmark Cards, Inc.,
Kansas City, MO 64141
Visit us on the web at www.Hallmark.com.

Editorial Director: Todd Hafer
Art Director: Kevin Swanson
Designer: Mark Voss
Production Artist: Dan C. Horton

Editorial development by Scott Degelman & Associates,
with additional writing by Lauren Benson.

ISBN: 978-1-59530-035-5

BOK4344

Printed and bound in China

to:

from:

A LOVE THAT LASTS

INSPIRING INSIGHTS FROM COUPLES MARRIED 50 YEARS AND BEYOND

Introduction

A friend of mine once decided to become a "student of love." Reading books by famous philosophers and religious thinkers, he sought to internalize some of the greatest thoughts on love ever written—and then put them into practice. He wanted to love others in a way that changes lives.

If I could put just one more book in his hands, it would be this one.

To me, few things are more life-changing than the love stories and insights shared by the 50 couples in this book—couples whose love has grown and endured over fifty years or more of marriage. These lifelong partners long ago turned the momentary sparks of newfound love into something real and "everyday" in the best sense of the word. (Something my own recently married friends are currently learning to do.)

In *A Love That Lasts,* you'll find couples who learned to combine humor with compassion, tenderness with strength, and enduring affection with some well-timed flirtation.

We're all students of the kind of love that, unlike momentary sparks and fireworks, will keep burning long and bright into the unknown future. Let's take some lessons from these men and women who know what it takes to keep laughter, passion, and love alive . . . for a lifetime.

A LOVE THAT LASTS CONTENTS

24 Let the good times "role."

25 Forgive.

26 Pick your battles.

27 Appearances are indeed deceiving.

28 Give and receive the gifts of love.

29 Set a few simple rules.

30 Manage conflict; don't let it manage you.

31 Keep your promises.

32 Share a spiritual journey.

33 Love has no fine print.

34 Go the extra mile for peace.

35 Get by with a little help from your friends . . . and family.

36 Know a higher power.

37 Absence makes the heart grow fonder.

38 Give a heartfelt (but humble) effort.

39 Take a chemistry class.

40 Keep on dancing.

41 Enjoy the simple things in life.

42 Don't sweat the small stuff.

43 Be kind.

44 Golden rule = golden anniversary.

45 Give each other room to grow.

46 Fight fair.

47 Forget about 50/50.

48 Don't go to bed angry.

49 Encourage; don't nag.

50 Enjoy the sounds of silence.

**Respect the institution,
but love the person.**

1

Tom and Judy Harper

MARRIED NOVEMBER 29, 1947

Much is said about the importance of "being committed to marriage." But for the Harpers, commitment to an institution—even one as time-honored as marriage—left them a bit cold. "I believe strongly in marriage," Tom says, "but I've always focused on being committed to Judy, to her as a person."

Judy adds, "Our love and passion is for each other. That's what inspires us every day and what has brought us through some very difficult times. Illness. Crumbling finances. The physical changes that age brings. What I've learned through it all is this: You can respect, even revere, an institution or ideal, but I've never been in love with one. I'm in love with Tom."

Brandon and Kelly Davis

MARRIED JANUARY 1, 1955

Kelly Davis has a simple answer to those who ask what attracted her to husband Brandon. "Why him?" she smiles. "He smelled the best." Kelly's answer might seem flippant, but it's not. She notes, "I figured if a guy took the trouble to smell better than all the rest of 'em, he'd probably be committed to being outstanding in other areas as well. And that's proven to be the case. For example, in addition to smelling great, he has one humdinger of a kiss!"

For his part, Brandon notes, "The whole reason I was so diligent about being a good-smelling gent was so I could attract someone like Kelly. Guess it worked."

In love,
the little
things count—
because they
are signs
of the bigger
things.

Remember that love
has the power to heal.

Ralph and Evelynn Sellers

MARRIED NOVEMBER 22, 1957

Being married for more than 50 years has helped Evelynn and Ralph Sellers truly appreciate the healing power of love. "In our early days together," Ralph recalls, "Evelynn made my heart hurt—in a good way. The love between us was so new, so strong, that it felt like more than my heart could take."

Today, Ralph reveals, life's challenges sometimes make his heart hurt, too—but not in a good way. "But," he says, "when that happens, Evelynn always makes my heart feel better. It's amazing. I know some people whose past hurts have kept them from beginning a relationship. I wish I could help them understand that a loving marriage might be just the thing they need to start healing those hurts."

4

Eric and Sara Phillips

MARRIED APRIL 21, 1951

Few burdens are as heavy to carry as the weight of someone's unrealistic expectations—especially when those expectations come from a person you love deeply. Early in their marriage, Eric and Sara expected each other to be adept at various aspects of marriage and running a household. They quickly became frustrated. "It was only after we acknowledged that we were both new at this," Sara recalls, "that we quit putting so much pressure on each other. We gave ourselves time to learn and grow."

Eric adds, "Once that pressure was off, we began to see how hard both of us were trying. That helped us appreciate each other's efforts, even when the actual results weren't perfect."

You'll find perfection

when you stop looking for it—or demanding it.

Marriage doesn't take care of itself.

Carol and Philip Bell

MARRIED JANUARY 10, 1958

Marriage is much like any other significant life endeavor; you get out of it what you put into it. After their wedding, the Bells threw themselves into their respective careers, Carol as a teacher, and Philip as a pastor. They assumed, in Philip's words, that "the marriage would take care of itself—kind of like autopilot, I guess."

Of course, that didn't happen. Carol's and Philip's careers got off to great starts, but the two of them found themselves losing their tempers, hurting one another's feelings, and having conversations in which neither party truly listened to the other.

"We learned the hard way," Carol says, "that a marriage that lasts is going to require as much dedication, time, and energy as a career—if not more. You have to really listen. You have to spend time together. You have to address problems head-on and work together to solve them."

"Once we started really working at our marriage," Philip says, "it began to thrive. That's why, more than fifty years later, we're still working on it."

Ken and Betty Achton

MARRIED DECEMBER 10, 1952

The book *Wake Up and Smell the Pizza* says it well: "When you keep score in a relationship, everyone loses." Winning and losing works when it comes to sports competition, or even in business. But in marriage, if you "win" at the expense of your partner, have you truly won? The Achtons, ever since they were married in Grenada, Kansas, more than 56 years ago, have sought to work for each other's happiness and fulfillment first.

"You must esteem the other person as more important than yourself," Ken says. "I'm not saying this is a secret to getting your own way in the end, but it is a secret to keeping your marriage together."

Remember
who is
Number 1.

(Hint: It's not you.)

Spend your efforts looking for ways to strengthen your marriage, not for escape hatches.

Harold and Norma Summers

MARRIED JUNE 20, 1955

In myriad ways, life today is better than it was back in the mid-twentieth century. But not everything has improved, according to Harold and Norma, whose union took place, appropriately, in Uniontown, PA. The Summerses cast a disappointed eye at today's complicated prenuptial agreements and easy-out divorces.

"They didn't give you an escape clause back in our day," Norma says. "We took marriage very seriously from the very beginning, and that's been important to us. We believe that if you continually have your eye out for the Exit signs, you're not going to be fully engaged—or fully committed—in your marriage. Quit fidgeting. Settle in and attend to the business at hand. You might just have the time of your life."

Ray and Brianna Morgan

MARRIED MARCH 12, 1957

If Ray had listened to his family and friends, he would have married Brianna's older sister. "Everyone was telling me that Bri's sister and I were 'perfect for each other!'" Ray recalls. "We were both gregarious and outrageous—and we were both performers."

Ray dated Brianna's sister a few times, and they enjoyed each other's company. However, it was the younger Brianna—quiet, introspective, and performance-phobic—who ended up capturing his heart. "Looking back on things," Ray notes, "Bri's sister and I would have clashed terribly. We both needed to be in the spotlight all of the time, and we both tend to dominate conversations. Bri and I, on the other hand, complement each other, balance each other. I've helped her become more comfortable in social situations, and she has taught me the immense value in closing my mouth once in a while to truly listen to others and contemplate the wonder that is life."

Sometimes
the matchmakers
are wrong.

Don't assume the "I love yous."

Wade and Stephanie Strock

MARRIED AUGUST 9, 1941

After years of marriage, a husband and wife might begin to assume their love for each other is understood. Pleas for a little assurance might be met with comebacks like, "Of course I love you; I'm still married to you, aren't I?" This is a little like assuming that a person can't be sick because there's medicine in the house. Loving words can be like medicine for the soul. They build a person up when he or she is sagging emotionally, physically, or spiritually. Sharing words or other expressions of love also strengthen you as a couple.

"I can be sinking in a quicksand of despair," Wade explains, "and a few loving words or a little love note from Steph can make me feel like I'm walking on air. I feel bulletproof. It's amazing the power that 'I love you' has."

So, whether you whisper it, shout it, write it, or even sing it, tell your partner today, "I love you."

10

Lionel and Carlita Robertson

MARRIED AUGUST 30, 1940

"How do you eat an elephant?" the question goes. The answer: "One bite at a time."

It's the same with marriage. A marriage, even one as enduring as the Robertsons', happens one day at a time. "When we were going through bad times—or having a big fight—I didn't say, 'Oh, no! How am I going to put up with fifty years of this?'" Carlita says. "I just focused on how to get through 'this hour, this day.' Otherwise, the whole thing can seem just too overwhelming."

Carlita, an avid quilter, has found a metaphor for marriage in her craft. "I look at marriage the same way I look at a patchwork quilt," she explains. "Every stitch is like a minute, every patch like a day. If you just focus on what's in front of you right now, after a while you have a big beautiful result, when all of those individual things are joined together."

Remember:
Fifty years happens one day at a time.

Common goals = common bonds.

11

Ervin and Nichole Standifer

MARRIED JULY 13, 1950

Certainly, couples don't need to do everything together, but they shouldn't live lives that are essentially separate, either. They need to share more than a bed and an occasional meal. Ervin and Nichole recently retired from their careers (salesman and receptionist, respectively) and they have been volunteering at their local church, serving as greeters and ushers, and helping with various refurbishment projects.

"Throughout our marriage, we found lots of projects to collaborate on," Ervin says, "such as home improvement. But on the career front, we worked in different fields, in different types of jobs. Now that we are retired, it is great to be volunteers, working together. We feel a little like we're working for the same company or playing for the same team."

"I highly recommend some kind of joint endeavors for all couples, whether you're volunteering together or taking karate lessons," Nichole concurs. "It really builds a sense of camaraderie between the two of you."

12

Georgette and Richard Berry

MARRIED MARCH 11, 1957

Maybe the Rolling Stones said it best: "You can't always get what you want." It's true about all aspects of life, including marriage. During their 50+ years together, the Berrys have faced a lot: layoffs, a serious illness for Richard, and several periods of bleak finances. These challenges put a strain on their marriage, but Richard and Georgette faced it all with a "bend, don't break" philosophy.

"It's just a fact," Richard says. "Life is not going to turn out exactly the way you hope. After all, no one hopes to become seriously ill, get fired, or have a marriage on the rocks. But it happens. So you have to make adjustments, make a Plan B—or even a Plan C."

Georgette notes, "I wish all young couples would be told that it's not a question of if you'll face some serious challenges in your life and marriage, it's a question of when. Then they'd be better prepared to adapt to change and to let go of the things that one simply can't control. Richard and I might not be as flexible physically as we once were, but mentally and emotionally we're dadgum ballet dancers!"

Flexibility:

It's not just for your
joints and muscles.

Be the first to say "I'm sorry."

13

Shelly and Cal Starr

MARRIED DECEMBER 24, 1956

"It was agonizing, sitting there in a tense house, waiting for the apology that I thought was owed to me," Cal Starr recalls. "That's how I dealt with marital conflict for the first couple of years. After a while, I had to ask myself, 'Exactly how long do you want to sit here, feeling tense and hurt and miserable?'"

As Cal ultimately learned, waiting for an apology or admission of wrong that we think is "owed" to us can be some of the loneliest and most frustrating waiting there is. "The sad thing is," Shelly explains, "Cal would be sitting in his chair, miserable, waiting for me to apologize, while I'd be upstairs, waiting for his apology. I honestly don't remember who first broke the impasse, but once that happened, it was like we had escaped from chains. Now it's practically a race to see who apologizes first."

"It's not important to determine who is more wrong or who offended whom first," Cal agrees. "The important thing is that both of us want to mend the damage that's been done. Both of us want to make peace. The sooner you get past all that stupid finger-pointing, the sooner you'll get to the making up!"

14

Quinton and Togi Barela

MARRIED FEBRUARY 14, 1954

The Barelas urge all couples to "come to their senses." But for them, the advice isn't what it seems at face value. Quinton and Togi, who were married in Hawaii on Valentine's Day, find it odd that many men and women don't use all of their senses in their married life. "You don't necessarily need to hear words to understand what your spouse is thinking or feeling," Quinton says. "In fact, you shouldn't rely just on words."

The Barelas have become experts in picking up on non-verbal cues—a knowing smile, a downcast face, a sluggish gait, a sense of tension or apprehension in the room. A clinging hug that says "I really need your support and love right now!" A slight quake in one's voice, a cue that says "I'm trying to hold it together, but I'm hurt and scared." Quinton and Togi know that when it comes to understanding your spouse and responding to his or her needs, what's not said is more significant than what is said. And, similarly, sometimes the context of a sentence or two outshines the words.

"Words are fine," Togi says, "but when you are truly tuned into your partner, you'll find that quite often you don't even need words to understand each other."

Listen
to what's
not being
said.

Never underestimate patience and empathy.

15

Zach and Rhonda Hollister

MARRIED JANUARY 9, 1958

Zach Hollister is a character. Fortunately, he knows it. One key to a successful marriage, according to Zach, is being aware of your idiosyncrasies—and being the kind of person who can put up with them. The woman who is driven to pursue a career on the Broadway stage. The man who insists on racing dirt bikes well into his 50s. The freelance artist whose income is as unpredictable as the weather.

A character like Zach can bring a lot to a relationship— excitement, adventure, energy, and passion—but all of that zing comes with a price tag. Finding the person who's willing to pay is the key. "I knew Rhonda was the right one for me," Zach says. "I knew she'd be up for the adventure that our life has been."

Rhonda has been putting up with Zach for more than 50 years now, and she says she wouldn't have it any other way. "Every other guy I dated was boring, compared to him," she says. "Sure, he's a handful sometimes, but he's a fun handful!"

16

Daniel and Sherry McCallister

MARRIED DECEMBER 24, 1956

Talk to a few long-happily married couples, and you're likely to hear comments like, "I married my best friend."

Count the McCallisters among this friendly bunch. For Daniel and Sherry, their union didn't grow out of a need for financial security, social status, or physical romance. As Daniel puts it, simply, "I needed a friend, and that's what I found in Sherry. That's what she found in me. For us, the romantic love stuff was just the cherry on top." Marrying out of friendship might not sound romantic or the stuff of movies and epic love poems, but it works. As the McCallisters are quick to point out, when you're struggling with your career or having major self-esteem issues, a candlelight dinner or vase of a dozen roses probably won't help all that much. Those are the times when you need a caring, sympathetic ear and some wise counsel.

"When times are tough," Sherry says, "the last thing I need is violin music and mood lighting. I need my best friend, and that's Daniel. And I know he feels the same way about me."

Don't just be lovers;
be friends.

There's magic in the intangible.

Reggie and Sarah Swinton

MARRIED OCTOBER 29, 1952

"What does she see in him?"
"I never pictured a guy like him with a girl like her."
"Have you ever seen a couple as odd as those two?"

How many times have you heard gossip like this? Or maybe a friend posed a similar question to you about one of your romantic choices. People look at things like differences in age, race, economic background, or personality type, then cast doubts about a relationship's viability. But couples like the Swintons have learned that sometimes it's the things that aren't immediately obvious—the intangibles—that make for an enduring relationship.

"I don't know how to explain it." Sarah says, "but there's just something about Reggie. Music always sounds better, sweeter, when we're together."

Reggie agrees. "When she's around," he smiles, "food is tastier, sunsets are more beautiful...heck, everything is just plain better." There is a place, of course, for lists and formulas and criteria when it comes to starting and building a relationship. But couples like the Swintons have learned that intangible magic can have a profound impact on the very tangible institution of marriage.

18

Jeff and Tolanda Jackson

MARRIED JULY 21, 1956

Great causes have brought many a couple together. A shared passion for teaching, serving the poor, or campaigning for a political candidate. For the Jacksons, who were married in Whitefish, Montana, the catalyst was something more mundane: green bean casserole.

"What first drew me to Jeff?" Tolanda recalls, "We both like green bean casserole." It's not the stuff of Shakespeare, but once Jeff and Tolanda found common ground in the all-important side-dish category, they moved on to other areas in which they shared interests and passion, such as a strong faith.

Marriages like the Jacksons' are a great reminder that those little shared quirks can sometimes mean a lot—and that it's worth noting who's checking out the same items as you on the buffet line or at the church potluck dinner.

A foundation
is made of
many small
bricks.

Know when to bend.

Anne and Edward Dean

MARRIED MARCH 23, 1940

Religion can be a source of a strong bond in a marriage; it can also be divisive, especially for an interfaith couple like the Deans. Anne is Jewish; Edward is a Protestant. During the early years of their marriage, each of them followed separate paths of faith, but when their first son was born, questions and debate arose. In whose faith would Michael be raised? The Deans listened to the opinions of their respective families but, in the end, told the in-laws that the decision would be theirs. After much discussion, they arrived at a compromise.

"My faith isn't unimportant to me," Edward explains, "but I'm not very active in my church. Anne, on the other hand, is passionate about her faith. And it was very important to her that our kids be brought up in the Jewish faith. I had always assumed that they'd go to my church, or at least split time, but my assumption was just based on tradition. I didn't have a deep personal conviction about it like Anne did."

As the couple discussed the matter, Edward became convinced of what he needed to do. And he's now been a proud onlooker at three Bar Mitzvahs.

"I'm not saying that our solution will work for everyone," Edward notes, "but it's what felt right for me. And Annie has been very gracious about having the boys participate in events at my church. Whatever path they end up following as adults, I know they'll do it with great purpose and thoughtfulness. I think the way we raised them will have a lot to do with that."

20

Joy and Alex Dominguez

MARRIED JULY 14, 1953

We all know the painstaking preparation one goes through for a date—especially a big date on Valentine's Day, New Year's Eve, or a birthday. Male or female, we want to look our best, smell our best, act our best. So every stray hair is plucked or trimmed. Every flaw is eliminated—or at least disguised. But no one can look perfect (or smell perfect) all the time. Especially in a long-term relationship in which two people share the same living space, including the same bedroom and bathroom.

So what happens when the defenses are down, the makeup is off, the morning breath reeks, the hair is messed up, and the stomach can't be sucked in any longer?

For Joy Dominguez, these questions separated Alex from all the other potential mates. "When I really thought about a life with someone," she explains, "it became very clear to me that I didn't want anyone but Alex watching me drool while I slept. Even with such a vulnerable, potentially embarrassing situation like that in my mind's eye, I felt OK about it—felt safe about it—when I thought of Alex. And I honestly couldn't say I felt that way about anybody else."

Alex found the same kind of acceptance and security in Joy, and that's why, more than 55 years later, they're still loving each other, morning breath and all.

Who can
you be
imperfect
with?

Don't forget your *meditation.*

21

Dom and Winnie Jansen

MARRIED MARCH 27, 1946

Have you ever been caught up in an argument that feels like going around and around the same racetrack—in hell? Even mature couples can get caught in the cruel game, visiting the same problems again and again. The only thing that changes is the level of frustration and anger.

"We're 'good' arguers," Dom explains, "but sometimes life's problems stretch you beyond your abilities and beyond your patience. Sometimes Winnie and I would get in an argument, and two hours later we hadn't solved anything. We were just spinning our wheels."

During the middle of one such conflict, Winnie suggested something she had heard from a friend. She and Dom retreated to neutral parts of their house to be quiet with their thoughts. For Winnie, this meant praying. For Dom, it meant meditating, to calm his nerves and quiet his heart—both literally and figuratively.

"We've found that some time of peaceful soul-seeking, reflection, and contemplation can work wonders," Winnie says. "Sometimes it provides the answers you need, right then and there. But even when it doesn't, it puts you in a better state of mind and spirit to find the answers. And, I know this sounds less than romantic, but sometimes you just need to get out of each other's face for a while."

Thomas and Mary Johnson

MARRIED JUNE 14, 1958

"Don't get me wrong," Thomas Johnson says. "I don't enjoy watching people around me getting divorces, especially when it happens to family members or friends. But at the same time, you'd be a fool not to notice the mistakes people make and try to avoid them in your own marriage." During their 50 years of marriage, the Johnsons have seen three primary mistakes that damage or end marriages.

1. Dishonesty. "You have to be able to trust each other," Mary says, "and you can't trust someone who's dishonest. Tell the truth, even about the little things."

2. Unresolved conflict or bitterness. "You can't let things fester," Thomas asserts. "That kind of thing will eat away at you, and it will affect how you treat your spouse. You'll be angry, impatient, cold, or whatever, without even intending to be."

3. Infidelity. "We've lost track," Mary says, "of how many marriages we've seen end because a man or woman had a fling out of anger, revenge, boredom, or curiosity. You can save yourself years and years of agony, guilt, bitterness, and more—just by staying true."

Learn
from
others'
mistakes.

Make your marriage better tomorrow than it is today.

23

Patricia and Allen Johnston

MARRIED APRIL 9, 1950

The Johnstons' mindset toward their athletic endeavors has helped their marriage. Patricia and Allen were collegiate athletes who have continued to compete in age-group tennis and running events, respectively. They noted how many of their peers strived to improve in their sports and their careers. However, when it came to marriage, maintaining the status quo seemed to be the standard goal.

"The only time we saw a couple really working hard on their marriage was when that marriage was in trouble," Patricia notes. "To us, that would be like training for a sport only when you were injured or out of shape."

So the Johnstons determined that they would pour effort into their marriage every day so that it would always be getting stronger. It's worked. Today they both say they are more in love than on the April day they were married—and that their marriage is the strongest it's ever been. "It might be OK to maintain your car or maintain your lawn," Allen observes, "but maintain a marriage? No way. You have to work at it, keep making it better. Believe me; you'll be glad you did."

24

Gene and Carrie Daugherty

MARRIED AUGUST 27, 1939

Sharing is an important part of any strong marriage, but the Daughertys maintain that sharing can be taken too far. Carrie explains: "You can't share everything all the time. You must have some clear-cut roles. When we first got married, we'd both say things like 'We need to open a savings account' or 'We need to make an appointment to have a will drawn up.' And guess what? 'We' never got around to doing anything!"

Eventually, Carrie and Gene learned the need for the definition and delegation of duties. Carrie managed the finances and paid the bills. Gene made the medical appointments and picked up prescriptions and other medications. Carrie sorted the mail. Gene made sure the car was properly maintained and tuned up.

"Having clear roles helps us both play to our strengths," Gene explains. "And it avoids all that useless bickering over whose turn it is to do what. Of course, there are some things that are the most fun when done together."

"Gene!" Carrie scolds.

Gene shrugs his shoulders. "I was just talking about dancing," he says.

Let the good
times "role."

Forgive.

Oliver and Hannah Smith

MARRIED JUNE 21, 1954

"I'm not gonna lie to ya," Oliver Smith says. "I used to hold grudges—big-time. We both did."

Hannah agrees, casting her eyes downward, "We both struggled to get past that feeling of being wronged. I would be bitter. Oliver would be distant and aloof—even after the requisite apologies and forgiveness."

Then the Smiths had a revelation, appropriately, in church. Their pastor quoted from St. Paul's first letter to the Corinthians, noting "Love keeps no record of wrongs."

"That hit me like a punch to the gut," Oliver recalls. "Because I was an expert bookkeeper when it came to all of the things Hannah did to hurt my feelings. So that was the turning point. You know, sometimes that verse is a pain in the neck to me, because there are still times when I'd like to have something to hold over her head, some kinda trump card to play when I really need it. But that's not love."

Hannah says, "We've pretty much gotten past the silly holding of grudges. Because when you hold on to a grudge, you can't hold much else. And, even after all these years, I'd rather hold Oliver any day."

26

Gene and Marie Krall

MARRIED JUNE 8, 1957

Finances. Household chores. Job-related pressures. Kid-related pressures. In-laws. Health challenges. The list of stressors to a marriage could fill a book. Combine big problems like the ones above with a few minor annoyances—a partner's snoring, a to-do list that never gets to-done—and the average married couple can find enough fuel to keep them bickering 24/7. The Kralls realized this truth about two years into their marriage, when they came to the end of a three-day weekend and noted they had spent virtually every waking hour complaining, kvetching, or commiserating about something.

"We realized we had just wasted a whole long weekend," Marie remembers, "and so the question came, 'Just how much of our married life do we want to throw away by bickering?'"

Obviously, major issues cannot—and should not—be avoided, but the Kralls learned that there is wisdom in showing one another a little grace once in a while. Today, with her husband now passed on, Marie says she is glad their 51-year marriage wasn't marred by constant "fussing and fighting."

"I miss Gene every day," she says, "but I'm glad that I'm living with so many happy memories instead of regrets over silly fights that, in the big picture, don't matter at all."

Pick your battles.

Appearances are indeed deceiving.

Jim and Neva Springston

MARRIED JUNE 10, 1936

What do you get when you combine a prim and proper schoolteacher with an irreverent, Navy vet auto mechanic? A marriage that endured for 67 years. Jim and Neva seemed like the classic odd couple. Neva always dressed impeccably and couldn't even bring herself to order "chicken breast" in a restaurant. Jim, on the other hand, practically lived in his mechanic's coveralls, sported permanent grease under his fingernails, and was fond of using a raunchy Navy saying or two—even around the grandchildren. But, despite all of the surface differences—which had casual onlookers shaking their heads—the Springstons shared deeper, if less visible bonds.

Their work ethic was virtually unmatched, even when they entered their 80s. They shared a deep faith in God and a steadfast commitment to their family. They thought nothing of driving 16 hours round-trip to see one of their grandchildren compete in a wrestling match. They also shared a love for travel, setting a goal to visit all 50 states together. Jim's death, due to cancer, stopped them just a couple of states short of their goal, but Neva isn't disappointed.

"Visiting all fifty states would have been nice," she says, "but that's not the most important thing. What means the most to me is the way we saw all those places—together."

Jay and Esther Hafer

MARRIED JANUARY 5, 1936

Every mature couple knows that there's much more to a marriage than the gifts one receives for Valentine's Day, a wedding anniversary, or birthday. But there are certain gifts that have a way of capturing what a marriage is all about.

Jay and Esther both came from humble backgrounds. They couldn't even afford a honeymoon. They married on a Sunday afternoon, and Jay went to work at 5:30 a.m. the next day. Seven years into their marriage, the Hafers still weren't able to afford a house. Jay continued his work on the seismograph crew, and Esther mended nylon pantyhose for people (at "fifteen cents a run"). Then, one day, Jay surprised Esther with a gift—a fashionable Bulova wristwatch. "I don't know how he did that for me," Esther says, shaking her head. "This was wartime; there were simply no watches available anywhere! I still have it. It's the only watch I've ever owned." Years later, while working as a secretary, Esther was able to return her husband's gesture. "In 1970," she says, "he was working as a hospital chaplain, making 500 bedside calls every week. I wanted to do something nice for him, so I bought him a ring with a small diamond in it—for one hundred dollars. I know it means a lot to him, because he still wears it." Esther says that these gifts, relatively grand gestures arising out of challenging times, epitomize their marriage. "It's been meager," she says, "but it's also been heaven."

Give and receive
the gifts of love.

Set a few simple rules.

Bob and Barbara Mayberry

MARRIED AUGUST 1, 1953

Relationships can be complicated, but the Mayberrys have seen their marriage not just survive but thrive during the past 55+ years. Their secret? A few simple rules, free of psychobabble and formula:

1. Trust each other—and be trustworthy.
2. Respect one another.
3. Be honest.
4. Keep no secrets from each other.
5. Strive for real love—beyond physical attraction and sex.
6. Don't sweat the small stuff.
7. Don't spend more than you can afford.

"There is nothing glamorous or revolutionary about the rules we've chosen to live by," Bob concedes. "I don't see the title of the next self-help best seller in there anywhere. But this is what has worked for us. We honestly love each other and care more deeply for each other right now than we ever have."

Georgia and Andrew Brennan

MARRIED JUNE 8, 1957

As a child, Georgia saw her parents fight all the time, while Andrew's parents rarely had visible conflict. Despite the different upbringings, Georgia and Andrew entered their marriage with the same perception: conflict should be avoided. So, when they found themselves stepping on each other's nerves, they retreated to neutral corners.

"Conflict was like the cockroaches in our first apartment," Andrew explains. "At first, we thought if we ignored the problem, it would just go away. But conflict and cockroaches are both hearty critters."

Frustrated, Georgia visited her pastor for advice. "I can't tell you how relieved I was," she recalls, "to hear that what we were going through was common. But I was surprised to hear him say we needed to argue." The pastor helped Georgia and Andrew see that conflict is something that needs to be resolved, not ignored. "I was clamming up when I was unhappy," she says. "But I found that these were times I needed to share my feelings or ask for Andrew's help."

Andrew nods his head in agreement. "It's funny," he says. "Sometimes we'll see a young couple walking hand in hand and I'll think, wow, those two must really be in love. Then again, any two people can gaze into each other's eyes. But can you argue constructively and respectfully? That's how you know you have a love that will stand the test of time."

"A love like ours," Georgia adds.

Manage conflict;

don't let it manage you.

Keep your promises.

31

Arthur and Galen Miles

MARRIED SEPTEMBER 8, 1957

Love works in mysterious ways, and the Miles' marriage is one example. "My first serious boyfriend had dumped me," Galen says, "and I was heartbroken." Eventually, Galen felt she was ready to give love another try, but she was wary.

She shared her fears with boyfriend No. 2, Arthur Miles. Rather than be offended or put off, Arthur made Galen a simple promise. "He promised me that he would never dump me," Galen smiles. "And he's been fulfilling that promise for more than fifty years now."

"I was very young when I made that promise," Arthur says, "but I was old enough to know about keeping your word. To me, my wedding vows were an extension of that earlier promise—a promise that I'm always going to keep."

32

Dave and Dee Clark

MARRIED AUGUST 22, 1954

The Clarks have traveled the world together. But they say that the most satisfying journey of their union has been a journey of faith. "We had been married about 14 years before matters of faith or religion were very important to us," Dee recalls, "but as we matured as people and experienced more of life, we both became convinced that there was more to life than just the physical realm. We both made a commitment to God, first me and then Dave, around the time of our 15th anniversary."

"I know that religion can cause tension in marriages," Dave says, "but it brought us closer together. Praying together—that is a very intimate, very sacred thing for two people to share." The Clarks pray together daily and spend hours every week discussing their respective journeys of faith.

"We don't agree on everything," Dee says, "so we are challenged—in a good way—by our differing perspectives. We had some intriguing, mind-stretching conversations, for example, during the most recent presidential election. We supported different candidates, but we respected how each other's candidate tried to balance his faith with his politics."

"Dee and I have a spiritual intimacy," Dave concludes, "that in some ways is even deeper than our physical or intellectual intimacy. We only wish we'd discovered it sooner."

Share
a spiritual
journey.

Love has no fine print.

33

Milt and Darlene S. [*]

MARRIED JANUARY 19, 1957

Most couples know that it's not a question of *if* a marriage will face storms and challenges, it's a question of *when*. Jobs are lost. Health goes south. Children rebel. And husbands and wives, being human, often respond badly to life's challenges. They go through periods of anger, depression, confusion, and unpredictability. Milt and Darlene have endured all of this and more.

It's common for a wife or husband to want out when the other partner is behaving poorly. "I never knew he had such a temper!" a wife might say. "She's put on so much weight," a husband might mutter to himself. Milt and Darlene have seen scenarios like these end marriages. But theirs has endured.

The secret? "Not just love," Darlene says emphatically, "but unconditional love. Milt and I didn't take it lightly when the minister said, 'For better or for worse.'" Milt and Darlene are quick to note that unconditional love does not mean ignoring a spouse's destructive behavior or attitudes, but it does mean helping each other grow as people rather than bailing out.

"If you truly love and understand someone, you stand by her," Milt says. "I'm thankful for Darlene's understanding and forgiveness, especially during the rocky times."

"And I'm thankful that you traveled an awful lot back then," Darlene adds with a wink.

* See editor's note at the end of this book.

34

Roberta and Robert Moody

MARRIED JUNE 3, 1938

The Moodys' early months of marriage were marked by the typical feelings of euphoria. "We were gaga over each other," Roberta says. "But after all that gaga stuff wore off, we realized just how much we enjoyed each other's company. We became the best of friends. I put up with Robert's snoring, and he put up with—well, whatever I might do to try to annoy him."

But even the best of friends quarrel. And what separates the lasting friendships from those more fleeting is how the combatants make peace. Roberta recalls one night when she was "madder than a hornet" at her spouse. Instead of sulking or returning anger for anger, Robert chose another path. In the middle of the night, he rose and went outside. Roberta had no idea what he was up to, and this nocturnal excursion only heightened her anger. Her anger subsided in the morning—when she saw the large bouquet of wildflowers her husband had collected for her.

"He picked all kinds of flowers for me," Roberta marvels. "In the dark. By morning those flowers were starting to get pretty sorry-looking, but I was touched. And, of course, I forgave him for whatever it was that made me angry. He was a true peacemaker. Robert is deceased now, but I hope the example he set will be helpful to other couples. He sure set a fine example for me."

Go the
extra mile
for peace.

Get by with a little help from your friends . . . and family.

35

Rich and Liz Eaton

MARRIED JANUARY 10, 1959

"My suitcases were laid out on the bed," Liz Eaton remembers. "I was ready to leave."

The Eatons had endured their first major blowup. Rich left for work and Liz called her best friend, Ann, to give her a ride to the bus station. Ann arrived promptly, but instead of helping Liz get away, she invited her friend to sit down and pour her heart out.

"Ann listened to me," Liz says, "without interrupting or judging. When I was done, she asked me if I really wanted to leave. If I still loved my husband. Those questions really brought me up short. What I really wanted to do was make peace with Rich."

Then Ann suggested something. She encouraged Liz to invite her older sister, a high school guidance counselor, to moderate a discussion between the newlyweds.

That evening, Liz's sister guided the couple as they sorted through their hurt and anger. She helped each of them see where they were at fault. She helped them realize anew how much they meant to each other.

"We laugh about it now," Liz says, "how I thought I was calling a getaway accomplice, but what I got was the voice of reason. And I can't count how many times my sister or one of my friends has been there for me—or for us. Whatever the challenge, it's so nice to be able to call in reinforcements. After all, that's what friends—and family—are for."

Mr. and Mrs. Bob McDaniel*

MARRIED JUNE 12, 1947

"I know some people might scoff," Bob McDaniel says, "but our marriage would have never endured without help from a higher power—and I don't mean my mother-in-law."

After marrying and establishing their first home, Bob and his wife found living in close quarters with a new companion can test one's patience beyond its capacity. Every bad habit, every personality quirk, is magnified. "Things got desperate pretty quickly," Bob says, "and we did the only thing we could think of—we prayed. We asked God for strength and patience and wisdom, and we believed—even though it was hard to believe—that he would rescue us."

Bob says the prayers were answered. "I don't know exactly how it happened," he says, "but somehow, day by day, we received the strength we needed to get by. Our faith in God was rewarded. Some people might chalk it up to our growing maturity or something like that, but we know there is no earthly explanation. And believe me, there's no way on earth my wife would put up with a guy like me without divine intervention!"

*See editor's note at the end of this book.

Know a higher power.

Absence makes the heart grow fonder.

Claude and Mary Stansberry

MARRIED JULY 31, 1946

The Stansberrys' wedding night was a short one, as Claude was roused at 5 a.m. by Mary's dad, who needed help spike pitching sheaves of oats on the family's farm. While he toiled all day, Mary prepared meals for neighboring farmers, enduring their wisecracks about the newlyweds and their abbreviated wedding night.

Later the couple began to settle into their life together, learning to adjust to one another's "quirks" and "oddities." "My mother-in-law ascribed most of the undesirable traits to me, while crediting Mary with the inherent compulsion to correct all of my shortcomings."

The most serious time of adjustment for the Stansberrys came when, in Claude's words, "I was removed from Mary's presence and inflicted on the U.S. Army." Upon his return from the service, Claude says he still had the same quirks and oddities—along with a few newly acquired ones. But once home, he found a very grateful and tolerant wife. "I didn't know if she had just decided to put up with me," he recalls, "or if the whole thing was part of a long-term strategy for my improvement. Eventually I learned that she had just decided to be tolerant, for which I am extremely thankful, as I am not yet perfect in all things."

The Stansberrys' advice to other couples is simple and a product of their gratitude for Claude's safe return from service. "You need to respect each other's space," Mary says, "and you really do need to accept who they are as a person."

Joseph and Ginnie Hathaway

MARRIED JULY 13, 1950

Some couples enter marriage with hearts full of confidence and heads full of advice from marriage experts, and there's certainly nothing wrong with that. To succeed in any endeavor, one needs confidence and knowledge. But the Hathaways' road to a successful marriage has been paved with some different stuff.

"This might sound weird," Joe says, "but we entered marriage with a lot of humility rather than a sense of boldness, and I think that's been one of the keys to our success. We didn't stand in the front of a church on our wedding day with this smug feeling that we were about to embark on the best marriage of all time—the kind that people make movies about."

As the years rolled by, the Hathaways' humility served them well. It made them eager to learn, from other couples as well as from various books and conferences about relationships. And it kept them from assuming that a happy marriage was an entitlement. "We understood from day one that this was something we'd have to keep working at," Ginnie says. "It wasn't going to happen by itself, just because we're such swell people."

Joe nods in agreement. "When I attend a wedding, I worry for those couples who stand up there with smug smiles on their faces. As far as I'm concerned, I'd rather see a clear-eyed man and woman whose faces reflect a look of humble hope."

Give
a heartfelt
(but humble)
effort.

Take a chemistry class.

39

Moriah and Benny Trujillo

MARRIED MAY 29, 1956

Moriah Trujillo had options when it came to romance. Many young men desired her company. But she knew Benny was her one-and-only, and the choice wasn't that difficult. It wasn't that he was the richest guy in town or the most athletic. But he had one important trait that set him apart from all of the other suitors in Salem.

"He was the only one who didn't irritate me," Moriah says. "We just clicked. There was something about his personality, his whole nature, that was a perfect fit for me. With everyone else, there was something about the way they talked to me or carried themselves that simply rubbed me the wrong way. Around Benny, though, my nerves were at peace. He's a class guy."

Moriah's advice for young lovers? "Don't focus on who looks good—or who you think makes you look good. Go for the person you truly enjoy just being around. Because that's what marriage is—a lot of being around each other. And if you don't have the right chemistry, something's gonna blow up."

40

Joshua and Elizabeth Hartman

MARRIED MAY 12, 1954

Many happily married couples have a hobby or pastime they enjoy sharing. For the Hartmans, it's dancing. "We've always enjoyed dancing," Joshua says, "ever since I tricked her into marrying me, back in Omaha. I just hoped that by the time she found out what I was really like, enough time would have passed so that she'd figure she was stuck with me."

"Actually, I tricked you into marrying me," Elizabeth corrects, "but you're right about the dancing. It was fun, and it helped me start liking you pretty good—around year 45 or so." The frequency of the activity has changed, but the Hartmans still enjoy dancing together, after 54+ years of marriage.

"Of course I still dance with her," Joshua laughs. "Just look at her. I dance with that pretty wife of mine every chance I get."

Keep
on
dancing.

Enjoy the simple things in life.

41

Roy and Fay Black

MARRIED FEBRUARY 28, 1943

Roy and Fay didn't have a car when they were married. They caught a ride with Roy's best man to their wedding. Roy took the bus to work. "I was a bit hamstrung when it came to taking my new bride out for a date," Roy says. "With no car, we weren't going very far." But sometimes romance can spring from humble circumstances.

Several times a week, the Blacks embarked on walking dates, visiting the park near their apartment, strolling through the neighborhood—always hand in hand. "We saw sunsets, children playing, hawks soaring, wispy clouds passing in front of plump full moons," Fay remembers. "I'll take that over any movie or restaurant."

Roy and Fay have his-and-hers cars now, but they still enjoy leaving the vehicles in the garage and venturing out on foot. "The sunsets are just as beautiful as ever," Roy says. "And so is Fay."

42

John and Janice Booker

MARRIED JANUARY 19, 1957

The Bookers have a saying that has served them well through decades of marriage: "You'll be just about as miserable as you decide to be."

"These days," Janice says, "I laugh when I think about the stuff that used to set me off—the noisy refrigerator, the broken cabinet door, the route John took when he drove places. And John had his little pet peeves about me, too."

Several years into their marriage, John and Janice realized that their many small irritations were taking the focus away from each other's emotional needs, their financial planning, and big-picture life goals.

"Learning to let all that little stuff go was a turning point for our marriage," Janice says. "We kind of put each other on notice. We'd catch each other going off about some dumb thing, and one of us would say, 'Is it worth it? Do we really want to spend the next four hours kvetching about...whatever?'"

Today, 51 years, three children, and two colon cancer surgeries later, the Bookers are grateful they knew what to let go—and when to let go of it. "It's such a gift," Janice says, "to live a thankful life and realize how blessed you are if you have a roof over your head, some food to eat, and your basic health—even if it took me two surgeries to get there. I don't know how much time John and I have left on this earth, but I do know that we'll spend it doing what's truly important. All couples would do well to do the same."

Don't
sweat
the small
stuff.

Be kind.

43

A.J. and Ann Jefferson

MARRIED JULY 18, 1946

It started with an eye roll from Ann's sister, Sue. "I was 'asking' A.J. to do an errand for me," Ann says, "and Sue, who was over for a visit, gave me this look. Then she said, 'Are you always this much of a grump to him? You didn't even say please.' I got defensive. I said something like, 'He talks to me the same way.' Then Sue gave me the look again. 'Well then,' she said, 'I feel sorry for both of you.' Those words really got to me. We'd been married only three years, and we were already taking each other for granted, not even showing the common courtesy we'd show to a stranger."

When the Jeffersons started paying closer attention to their interactions, they were shocked at how much sarcasm, indifference, and, sometimes, downright rudeness had crept into their language. They made a vow to show each other more kindness, more grace.

"It makes a world of difference when Ann asks me for something in a voice that's sweet and polite," A.J. says. "And I know she appreciates it when I don't get all bent out of shape when she asks me to repeat something I just said. It's ironic, you know. Sometimes your own spouse is the last person you'll show a little kindness to. He or she should be the first."

44

Rick and Jean Martin

MARRIED MARCH 12, 1957

"I was raised on the Golden Rule," Rick Martin says, "and I've done a pretty good job of living by it. With one notable exception: my poor wife. With everyone else, I was treating them the way I'd like to be treated, but when it came to Jean, I was treating her whatever old way my mood dictated. And often I was cranky and tired—partially from being so darned nice to everyone else."

Rick says he had a revelation one day when a co-worker at his office was rude to him, and he silently wondered, How would you like it if I treated you that way? "I'm not sure how that incident at the office led my thoughts toward Jean," Rick says, "but it did." Before he went home that night, Rick made a list of how he'd like to be treated. With respect, kindness, patience, thoughtfulness, gratefulness, forgiveness, and love. He made a practice of reviewing the list every night before returning home to Jean. She noticed the change right away.

"I remember that she asked me, 'Why are you being so nice to me?'" Rick recalls. "She was actually suspicious. That cut me to the quick. I realized how much I needed to change."

But Rick did change, as evidenced by the message Jean wrote in her 50th anniversary card to him. In part it said, "Thank you for treating me like your princess."

Golden rule = golden anniversary.

Give each other room to grow.

45

Mark and Pam Cooper

MARRIED APRIL 21, 1951

To couples like the Coopers, there is a world of difference between marrying someone, then trying to change him and allowing the one you married room and encouragement to grow. "From day one," Pam says, "I accepted Mark for who he was. But that didn't mean I didn't want the best for him and from him."

A decade into their marriage, Mark found himself stressed out and creatively stifled in his sales career. It affected his health and his marriage. He wanted to return to school, to earn his teaching credentials. He hesitated sharing his thoughts with Pam, but one night, in frustration, he did.

"It was the best thing for him," Pam explains, "and in the long run, it was the best thing for us." She helped Mark choose a school where he could earn his teaching credentials, and increased her hours at the office. A few years later, when Pam became a serious runner, Mark had the opportunity to return the favor, as he trained with her, supported her at races, and shouldered a larger share of the household duties when she was training for major events, such as triathlons and marathons.

"Our marriage vows talked about 'for better,'" Mark says, "and to us that transcends circumstances; it means helping each other be better people, helping each other reach personal and professional goals."

46

Lynn and Dean Larson

MARRIED MARCH 7, 1959

"You can't be in close quarters with someone for half a century and not trample on each other's nerves occasionally," Lynn Larson observes. "I hear couples who say, 'We never had one argument in fifty years,' and I wonder what drugs they were on. If you're passionate about your relationship—and each other—the fur's gonna fly sometime."

The Larsons contend that conflict can be constructive, if it's handled maturely. After a few heated arguments early in their marriage, they began to work on a list of rules for a "fair fight."

1. Focus on the problem, not the person. Don't get cruel or personal. (OK: "You didn't mow the lawn as you promised you would." Not OK: "You're an unreliable, lazy slob.")
2. Focus on the issue at hand—don't bring up past grievances.
3. Listen.
4. Listen some more.
5. Affirm your partner and your love for him or her.
6. Take some time to cool down if needed. (Take a long walk. Listen to some music. Breathe.)
7. Don't be too proud to call upon a referee if needed. (The referee might be a counselor, psychologist, religious leader, or "God Himself," according to Dean.)

"Because we've insisted on our fights being fair," Lynn says, "our marriage has been better than fair. It's been excellent!"

Fight fair.

Forget about 50/50.

Barb and Tim Strawberry

MARRIED OCTOBER 29, 1952

"I've heard it said that marriage is a 50-50 proposition," Tim Strawberry growls. "Well, where I went to school, 50 percent was a failing grade. And you couldn't find some other schmuck who got a fifty, add his score to yours, and start crowing, 'Look at me; I got 100 percent!'"

The Strawberrys sometimes speak to young couples, and they always encourage their audience not to focus on carrying "your share" of the load. "You must be willing to carry the whole load," they assert. "That needs to be your attitude."

Barb and Tim say that being willing to serve each other, in ways large and small, has been a hallmark of their long and happy marriage. "We don't demand that we meet each other halfway," Barb notes. "We both strive to be willing to go the whole way. Give our complete effort. If either of us sees something that needs to be done, we just up and do it. And I'll tell you, effort isn't a pain in the neck when it's flowing from the love that is in your heart."

"We've always been willing to go the extra mile for each other," Tim concludes, "and I think that's why we're miles ahead of most of the other couples we know."

48

William and Wendy Collins

At their wedding, the minister said to William and Wendy, "Don't go to bed angry." It seemed like reasonable advice. But once the stresses of marriage began to wear them down, the advice seemed impossible. In the heat of battle it made them angrier to feel pressured to settle an argument before bedtime. Frustrated, they returned to their minister. He listened as the couple accused him of giving them an impossible mission. Then he spoke gently, "Think back to what I said. I didn't say, 'Solve every argument and feel completely good about everything—and do it before 10 p.m.'"

"Yes, you did," William snapped.

"No," came the answer. "I merely said to avoid going to bed angry. You don't have to solve your problem before the lights go out. You don't even have to feel great about each other. You just need to find a way to let the anger dissipate. That might mean calling a temporary truce or taking a long walk to cool off."

The conversation was a revelation to the Collinses. "We'd been putting all this pressure on ourselves to solve every problem and feel perfect bliss—or we weren't allowed to sleep," Wendy explains. "All we really needed to do is make sure we didn't hit the pillows with hearts and heads full of anger. It's not easy, but it's doable. And if you avoid going to bed angry, the problems are so much easier to deal with when morning comes."

Don't go to bed angry.

Encourage;
don't nag.

49

Doug and Marie Larson

MARRIED APRIL 30, 1957

Part of intimacy is the security and freedom to help your partner grow and improve. There is a fine line between nagging and encouragement, of course, and the Larsons have a keen sense of where that line is.

"You can't be petty about things," Marie Larson explains, "but a husband and wife can really help each other improve—in large and small ways. For example, I noticed that Doug, who is very shy, struggled to look people in the eye. I pointed this out to him, gently noting that some people might assume he was dishonest or aloof. He understood and improved his eye contact right away. (It helped that I reminded him of what beautiful eyes he has.) As for me, I had a tendency to talk with my mouth full of food. I am very manners-conscious, but this was a total blind spot of mine. I am sure lots of people noticed, but it took Doug to point it out to me. Now I do a better job of keeping my yap shut if I'm working on a burger or something."

"If you continually affirm each other," Doug says (looking his interviewer squarely in the eyes), "it gives you permission to gently note ways you can help each other grow. Marie and I are better people for the way we've encouraged each other over the years. I don't know what I would have done without her—probably wander around with my eyes downcast and my fly open."

50

Shelly and Jedd Thomason

MARRIED JUNE 6, 1953

The Thomasons don't discount all the focus on a couple's need to communicate with one another. Good communication has been a key to their long union. But Jedd realized he and Shelly were right for each other one day when the talking ceased.

"You hear a lot about 'uncomfortable silences,'" Jedd explains, "and I had my share of those on dates. You feel like you have to keep talking or have music playing or have some form of entertainment going on. Because it gets awkward when things go silent. But it was different with me and Shelly, right from the start. We could have a great conversation or something, then just sit peacefully and silently, simply enjoying each other's company. To this day, she's the only one I can sit with when the TV is off. I tend to get antsy around other people, but not around her."

"I think those quiet moments are a true test of a relationship, any relationship," Shelly says. "You know you're with a soul mate when neither of you feels pressured to keep the noise going. All of that stuff can be a distraction. But I'm at perfect peace, just sitting in a quiet room with my husband, enjoying a comfortable silence. To me, it feels like home."

Enjoy the sounds
of silence.

Editor's Note

It's appropriate that a book about a love that endures for years took years to research, compile, and edit. In most cases, we were able to talk with both members of each of the couples featured in these pages. However, at times, we relied on the recollections of a couple's surviving member, a couple's children and close friends, and/or journals and diaries that were made available to us. Also, in rare instances, we encountered a couple eager to share their story but wary of revealing their full names, the place and date of their wedding, or other identifying biographical information—due to concerns about identity theft, which, sadly, had victimized them in the past. To respect these couples' privacy, we have avoided using their full names and been intentionally vague about background information.

If you have enjoyed this book,
or if it has touched your life in some way,
we would love to hear from you.

Please write:

Book Feedback
Hallmark Cards, Inc.
2501 McGee Street
Mail Drop 215
Kansas City, MO 64108

Or e-mail:
booknotes@hallmark.com

Look for Gift Books from Hallmark wherever
Hallmark Cards and other products are sold.